More Rhyme and Reason

Poems and anecdotes from the heart of Cornwall

Clarice Westlake

Clarice Westlake

CW00530288

www.withrhymeandreason.org

To Tom,

my life's companion.

Contents

The Master's Voice

A rhyme is a curious creature
With a mind that's entirely its own
It lives in your head
Most times it plays dead
Then pops up when
You think you're alone

A rhyme can come easy
Just flow from the heart
Or taunt you and tease you
When the words just won't start

You may think you control it
That just isn't true –
For the rhyme is the master
And the master rules you

The Seasons of My Life

Give me a little longer Lord, I'm not ready yet to go
I can't go in the wintertime, for I love the touch of snow
I love the crunch beneath my feet, the flakes upon my face
I need a little longer, Lord, in this beloved place
Let me watch the little snowdrops push their heads out of the snow
Give me a little longer, Lord, I'm not ready yet to go

Give me a little longer, Lord, I can't go for a while
I can't go in the springtime, and miss the primrose smile
When all the world is full of gold, the gorse upon the hill
And my heart and soul are singing at the scent of daffodils
Oh, let me watch the newborn lambs as I sit upon a stile
Just a little longer, Lord, I can't leave for a while

Give me a little longer, Lord, before I come to You
I can't come in the summertime, when all the sky is blue
And the sun is warm upon my back as I sit beneath a tree
And dream with my love in the garden to the song of a bumble bee
There are so many precious times, so many things to do
Give me a little longer, Lord, before I come to You

Give me a little longer, Lord, I'm not ready yet to go
I can't go in the autumn time when all the world's aglow
When all the leaves are red and gold and there's crispness in the air
Should the hazel nuts need picking, how can I not be there?
To smell a bonfire on the breeze and watch the sunsets glow
Give me a little longer, Lord, I'm not ready yet to go

But take me gently when You come, take me unaware
Take me when my eyes are closed, when I know not You are there
So that when once more they open, as You have vowed they will
They will not mourn this world at all, but see greater beauty still

The Goalie
or
Hooray for England

He gasped in great excitement
They've sent for me to play
They've said they really want me
Can I come right away?
I thought that I would be too old
I'd never play again
But the old ones are the best ones
They've made that very plain

He dived to left, he dived to right
And tipped balls o'er the bar
Then saved two certain penalties
His greatest game by far
And when the game was over
They cheered him off the field
And carried him up shoulder high
To get his winner's shield

He said "I feel so very proud
I can't believe it's true
That I should play for England
Now I am seventy-two"
And he turned towards his lady wife
Who'd been kicked till she could scream
And as he rubbed his sleepy eyes
Recalled his lovely dream

Two Thousand – Minus One

Welcome all to '99, and a happy, blest New Year
The last one of the century, the new millennium's here
We're on the final countdown, just one more year to wait
Do you think that we'll be ready for that long awaited date?

We know the nation's gearing up – we've even got a dome!
So our village must have something, maybe a garden gnome?
Perhaps a better thing would be twin statues on the green
Of Reverend T and Reverend C to remind us what this means

That two thousand's not a random date, just hit upon by Man
To keep our diaries up to date, but when Christendom began
Perhaps we've been a little slow to take the message in
But maybe the new millennium is a good time to begin?

Wouldn't it be nice to think we'd start with our slates clean
All past grudges wiped away as though they'd never been?
Those little things that hurt us once, but that was long ago
It's a good time to forget them, forgive, and then let go

The people and the family who shared our homes and hearts
But now have drifted far away, our lives light years apart
What better time to take the plunge, not waste our time and wait
Just say "I love you, please come home before it gets too late"

The millennium magic's working, and we want to join the fun
So hand in hand and laughing, two thousand, here we come
It's time to let our hair down, and spread some sunshine too
Think of things we've never done, but always wished to do!

Like hug a passing granny, and kiss her on the cheek
She may pretend you're shocking, but she won't wash for a week
And smile at the tax inspector, he's only human too
Then, as he strips your wallet, he'll smile right back at you

The old millennium's passing, the new a book untold
In which is writ our futures, whatever they may hold
It's all there waiting for us, so give three hearty cheers
Here's to a new millennium, may it last a thousand years!

My Search

They said my Lord has risen, to dwell in heaven above
Though he had died upon the cross, to save us with His love
They said that though my Lord had gone, His spirit was still here
But I had never seen him, had never felt Him near

So I went upon a journey, to see how this could be
If I travelled far enough, perhaps he'd come to me
I searched for Him in the city, but I couldn't find him there
No matter where I looked for Him, the streets were cold and bare

I sought Him in the country where the grass was fresh and green
But I could find no trace of Him, no sign where He had been
I found no trace in sea or sky, though I journeyed far and near
There was no use in trying, my Lord could not be here

So I gave up all my searching, let all my doubts depart
And that was when I found him, my Lord lives in my heart

In truth, the search continues

Surf Babe (circa 1954)

I was the lissom surfer you saw on Tolcarne beach
With tiny waist, and glossy hair, with just a touch of bleach
On shapely legs that couldn't wait I'd run toward the sea
For hour on hour we'd ride the waves, my belly board and me

We'd ride them in the sunshine, we'd ride them in the rain
And when the other folk came out we'd go back in again
It was the perfect marriage between my board and me
A hunk of hefty plywood – and a fifties surf queen bee

I am the aged surfer you see on Tolcarne beach
With bulging waist and silver hair, and suspiciously white teeth
On stiff veined legs, at stately pace I stroll toward the sea
And flop down on my belly board, Queen Mother not queen bee

The beach is getting longer of that there is no doubt
It's just a few yards riding in, but ten miles walking out
It must be global warming, that's very plain to see
So we're hanging up our water wings, my belly board and me

I'll sit down in my rocking chair and dream of days gone by
While gazing at my brand new shelf, made of well-seasoned ply

Waterworks Anonymous
(a tale in terrible taste)

I had a lovely birthday, just the other day
Great cause for celebration, or so the pundits say
I've had my three score years and ten
That we are told's our due
But here's a cautionary tale
That I must tell to you

Now really, I'm so grateful, of that there is no doubt
But age brings little problems that no-one talks about
Like the waterworks get dodgy, and 'night trips' are a must
No, shall I go or shall I wait, but thank God I made it – just!

A visit to the cinema requires a 'recce' first
Now just where is that lavatory, my bladder's fit to burst!
My word that is a scary scene, but I dare not jump with fright
Or cough or sneeze, NO, none of these, just sit here very tight

When going on a lengthy trip, you plan before you start
And note all service stations, just half a mile apart
The liquid intake's limited, don't give that drink a glance
We'd better 'go' now, just in case, best not to take a chance

Where years ago you ruled your works and made them wait for hours
Now they are in complete control and say "Revenge is ours"
But do not think you are alone, if your friends are seventy, too
Just look for signs of suffering – there's one not far from you

Post script
But if you've not yet reached that age
And you're chuckling now with glee
It's following right behind you
And gaining fast – YOU'LL SEE!

To a Small Grand Daughter

Come along my little girl, come and hold my hand
And off we'll go together into a magic land
It doesn't take you too long to go, you needn't wander far
Just sit and listen for a while, and whoopsy there you are!

You're in a land where teddies talk, what tales they have to tell!
Where dollies dance, and pixies prance, and magic creatures dwell
You might just see the fairies, there upon the hill
Dancing in the moonlight – if you stay very still

So come with me, my little girl, come and hold my hand
And off we'll go together into that magic land
I'll take you where your Daddy went, when he was small like you
Where he and I spent happy hours, and you and I shall too

Not all can find this country, just a lucky few
But we shall always share it, your Dad and me and you

The Attic Mouse
(a little rhyme for little people)

The mouse in the attic is playing a game
His little feet scamper again and again
He runs to and fro, does a skip and a hop
Do you think that little mouse ever will stop?

He lives just above, in the roof of our house
And plays half the night, that wee attic mouse
Just when the rest of us climb into bed
He decides to do handstands and cartwheels instead

But now it's near morning and all has gone still
What is mousy doing? Come peep, if you will
Together we creep up the old attic stairs
Oh look, he's all sleepy and saying his prayers

Now he climbs into bed, and we hear a faint snore
Attic mouse is asleep now, hush, come close the door

Sweet dreams, attic mouse

Sweet Memories

When I shall die, don't wear sad black dresses
Don't buy me flowers done up in tight rings
Just pick me some violets fresh from your garden
Remember me with the simplest of things

Hold hands and smiling, sing me a love song
Remind me of sweet times, and mem'ries we share
Give me your blessings, then go home together
And I'll rest content with the love you leave there

My Best Beloved

How much do I love you?
I do not know
For love has no limits
I love you so

How great is my love for you?
You cannot know
How big is the universe?
I love you so

'Till when shall I love you?
How can we know?
How long is eternity?
I love you so

The Monday Washday Blues

Crack of dawn in 1930, and in a place not far away
Every wife and every mother prepares for Monday's Washing Day
Gets dressed up in hessian 'wrapper' then puts the water on to heat
They've filled the 'copper' up on Sunday, now light it up with wood and
peat

In the 'linney' they have 'smutties' picked last Friday on the moors
Nicely dried just right for stoking, must boil up old Granfer's drawers
Down comes the zinc bath from its station, hung outside upon a nail
Then Mother sets the day in motion as she fills it with her pail

First comes the cold, and then the hot
Be careful dear don't use the lot
All the laundry's neatly sorted, first the 'best whites', slightly soiled
Get the soap and 'Rinso' treatment, then in the copper to be boiled

'Second' whites, the towels and bedding, sheets and shirts all get their turn
Still the housewives pound and pummel, till their faces sweat and burn
Dip the water – stoke the copper – stir and poke the washing down
Fetch cold water for the blue bath, squeeze the blue bag, swish it round

Now the rinsings and the blueings, then through the mangle it must go
Collars stiff starched, and the aprons, gaily on the line they blow

A cup of tea, a little gossip, and then the ladies start again
On hands and knees they scrub their houses, can't throw hot water down
the drain
Tomorrow morn will bring the ironing so long as it don't start to rain
But for now their journey's over, till Monday morning dawns again

Two Sides of a Coin – the Camel Trail by Day

All along the Camel Trail, the people come and go
Like busy ants they hurry and scurry to and fro'
It never stops from dawn to dusk, a conveyor belt in motion
A dirt track road, no highway code, just non-stop locomotion

First there come the Sunday strollers, gently ambling on their way
With dogs and kids, and Gran and Grandpa, out to have a quiet day
'Ting-a-ling', impatient cyclists try to pass in double file
Gran moves very slightly sideways, false teeth clenched behind her smile

Stalwart walkers, toting rucksacks, with hiking boots and woolly socks
Stride towards the beckoning footpath, like greyhounds to the starting
blocks
Plastic bottles full of Britvic, healthy bars of nutty chews
Eager to display their fitness, they do not even see the views

Ageing couples riding tandem, short of breath and broad of beam
Furrowed brows in concentration, struggle on towards their dream
Mile on mile they peddle onwards, faces set against the pain
Left, right, left, twin bottoms wobble, did ever Lycra take such strain?

Corduroy clad serious cyclists, rear ends higher than their face
Mums and Dads with kids in trailers, for one and all there is a place
All kinds, all creeds, and all conditions are mirrored in this motley throng
United in their great endeavour, they meet, and greet, and pass along

One thing they will have in common, young and old and in between
Strangers to each other, maybe, but members of a special team
For years to come, to all and sundry, they will tell the glorious tale
Of how they strove, and how they conquered –
The day they did the Camel Trail

Two Sides of a Coin – the Camel Trail by Night

It's Peaceful Night on the Camel Trail
The scurrying bikes have gone to their rest
And the hikers disappeared to distant homes
The path lies empty –
No bells ringing, no voices shout, and nature claims her own

On the horizon a fishing boat slides silently past Doom Bar
Just a moonlight shadow on the sea
In the estuary a cormorant makes one last low sweep
Then, it too, is gone

Far away across the water a sea bird calls, alone and lonely
One by one the lights are dimmed
The heronry falls silent
All is still and Padstow sleeps

The Fly on the Wall

When I have gone to that sweet place
Where all good Grannies go
Don't sit around and cry for me
Just look toward tomorrow

Remember all the times we've laughed
At flies upon the wall
And "Granny's watching us again!"
Well that won't change at all

Sometimes you'll hear a merry buzzzzz
And look towards the wall
And there that little fly will be
Smiling at you all

Wherever you may go in life
Whatever you may do
That little fly will follow you
And she'll look after you

She'll watch you on your happy days
And notice when you're sad
And always she will love you
Just as she always has

The Candle

It was quiet in the church today
As we all remembered you
The way you looked, the way you spoke
The things you used to do

We wondered where you'd really gone
And why you had to go
We thought how we would miss you
And wished we'd told you so

Three candles burned so brightly
As if to light your way
But one just flickered sadly
And seemed to fade away

We watched the failing candle
And mourned its dying light
But suddenly the flame burst forth
A beacon, shining bright

And we wondered, as we watched it
The joyous, dancing glow
Was that when you saw the face of God?
And hoped that it was so

Green Apples

Today I remembered the cottage
And wished that was where I could be
Safe in the home where I lived as a child
With the warmth of its arms around me

Sleeping once more in the old feather bed
With my father's firm step on the stair
And just for a moment I fancied
I could feel his kind hand stroke my hair

Today I wandered the winding path
That led to our old apple tree
And the red apples that were always my sister's
And the green ones she said were for me

How I hated my sour green apples
How I cried that it just wasn't fair
Till a grown-up came to the rescue
And she laughingly tossed me my share

Tonight I might dream of the cottage
And others may follow me there
To play once again in the sunshine
Once more hear the step on the stair

I shan't mind if I get the green apples
I shall know that it's only a game
And I'll laugh and enjoy the dear memories
Till morning returns me again

Easter Day

It's Easter Day and choirs are singing
"Christ the Lord is risen today"
In the belfry bells are ringing
Listen now, hear what they say.
Pain is over, sorrow banished
Lenten grief all washed away,
Now's the time for celebration
Oh, happy, happy Easter Day.

Easter eggs in brilliant boxes
By loving parents stored away
White-iced cakes with yellow chicks on
Have all been waiting for this day.
Little faces wrapped in chocolate
Little fingers bathed in goo
Offer half-chewed bits of sweetie
"Here you are Mum that's for you".
Mummy, with a moved expression
Accepts the offer with great glee
"Thank you darling that was lovely
I think I'll keep it for my tea."

It's Easter Day and joy is bubbling
All around, so plain to see
The faithful say "My Lord has risen"
The hopeful think "Please let it be".
Let nothing spoil this Easter pleasure
Let love and laughter have their way
Choirs keep singing, bells keep ringing
Oh happy, happy Easter Day!

We Are With You

When you felt that first cold fear, we were fearful with you
When you waited and watched in the dark of the night, in spirit we sat
beside you
When you had to say your last goodbye, we grieved with you
And as you cried, our arms ached to comfort you

Now you are alone and the world is a cold and frightening place, with no-
one walking by your side
So, as you step into your altered life, let us hold your hands and steady you
And if you stumble on the way, lean on us and we will keep you firm

We cannot ease your grief, or take away your pain
We can only stand close beside you, and wait with you until the clouds
begin to break
And when first you smile again, at a happy memory of days gone by, our
hearts will sing for you
And when you turn your face once more toward the sun
We shall bask with you in its warmth, and give thanks

Granny Rowe

Granny Rowe was short and dumpy
Small of face and fine of hair
In the first years of my childhood
Granny Rowe was always there
She was Gran, but also mother
To my sister and to me
Keeping house for son and children
She ruled, lovingly, all three

Granny Rowe was quite a lady
In her own endearing way
Much more keen on 'power dressing'
Than on house work any day!
Off she'd go to Church on Sunday
Fox fur draped around her chest
Patent shoes, and rings a-jingle
How she loved her Sunday best!

Gran was also quite conceited
In a most delightful way
Went into a state of panic
When she found a hair of grey
This couldn't happen, mustn't happen
What would all the neighbours think?
So she applied a pot of lotion
Lost the grey and turned bright pink

Granny Rowe was superstitious
Every travelling gypsy's dream
Asked for "Cup of tea my dearie"
She would add splits, jam and cream!

She believed we would be lucky
If she bought a gypsy charm
Clothes pegs, lace and lengths of ribbon!
Just to keep us safe from harm

Gran Rowe thought her heart was dodgy
Or that's the tale she told to me!
Only one thing kept her going
Sadly, a necessity!
Brandy from the 'Plume of Feathers'
Just a teaspoon twice a day
She didn't like it, no, of course not
But Gran was stoical that way!

Off we'd creep to 'Plume of Feathers'
Guilty partners side by side
Tap, tap, tap, on Feathers' side door
Someone's passing, quickly, hide!
Bottle tucked in inside pocket
Happy on our homeward way
Gran smiles graciously at neighbour
"We thought we'd take a walk today"

I take my happy memories
And I hug them to my heart
And try not to blame the people
Who said that we must part
How much I missed my Granny
No-one else can ever know
For she was all the world to me
How I wish I'd told her so

Observation:
It is quite possible that Gran really believed she needed the Brandy, along with the Phyllosan, Wincarnis, Carters Liver Pills, Californian Syrups of Figs, Andrews Liver Salts etc, etc, etc…

To My Valentine

Do you remember long ago
When first you were my Valentine
How life stretched forward endlessly
The world forever yours and mine?

The grass was green, our love was new
And so, we thought, 'twould ever be
The sun for us would always shine
No cloud could threaten you and me

We ran through fields of daffodils
No time to stop and wonder then
For we had many miles to go
The future beckoning again

So life moved on, how fast it sped
So quick we didn't see it go!
The mirror says we're old and grey
But I shall never see us so

We stroll through fields of daffodils
And pause a while, drink in the view
And as the miles grow shorter now
I thank the Lord I still have you

The future still keeps beckoning
Your hand stays tightly wrapped in mine
Our journey is not finished yet
My one, my only, Valentine

What a Wonderful World

Have you seen what's happening under our noses?
The creatures all strutting and striking strange poses!
Have you seen that the Grandpas are suddenly spry
With a spring in their step, and a gleam in their eye?
Have you noticed the catkins all fluffy and furry
Bursting their buttons they're in such a hurry

Down in the meadows the flowers are all springing
While up in the treetops the birds are all singing
And frantically rushing to finish their nest
With moss of top quality – must have the best!

Over our land the excitement is growing
Just look at the Celandine, see how it's glowing
All nature is joining the happy parade
Just look at the wonderful world He has made
Come on, let's join in, turn cartwheels and sing
The miracles happened again, look, it's Spring!

In Flanders Fields

They came again to Flanders fields
Where once, in mud, red poppies grew
And young boys grew, too soon, to men
Who vowed they would not come again
But back they came, though God knows why
Just one last time, to say goodbye
And as we watched we couldn't know
How they had suffered long ago

But we marvelled that, so long ahead
They remembered still their friends, the dead
Their names, their faces, haunt them still
Their memories live and always will
But we, the young, can never know
That comradeship of long ago
When stranger was your closest friend
And friend your brother, to the end

How could we know? For they did not tell
Those men who trod the road to hell
Did they feel guilt that they survived
When others, just as good, had died?
Did they blame their God for all the pain
For blood and fear, for mud and pain?
Or think it part of some great plan
That through fire shall come a better man?

We shall not know, they will not tell
Those men, who trod the road to hell
But still we feel, when we see their eyes
The depth, the pain, of their sacrifice
As they look at the grave of Bill or Joe
And whisper "Yes I knew him long ago"

The Parish Outing

Didn't we have a luverly time
The day we went to Buckfast?
Off on the coach, bypassing Roche
Oh, how the time seemed to fly past!

Arrived at the Abbey, all sticky and flabby
And longing for fruit cake and tea
Had a cup of Darjeeling, got that holiday feeling
So off we went on a gift-buying spree

The bus left at four, we still wanted more
But we all trundled back 'good as gold'
The monks were untroubled, their profits had doubled
You should have seen all that they'd sold!

The folks were all singing till our ears started ringing
They kept going most of the way
The bus was so cosy that Martin got dozy
But then he had had a hard day

Back to Lanivet, where 'quick as a trivet'
We were eating with all might and main
We'd had a great day, and laughed all the way
Please when can we do it again?

The Farm Evening

You all know farmer Blewett, you must have heard of he
He's always on the wireless, and sometimes on TV
If Radio Cornwall want to 'knaw' 'bout farming and such things
They know that they'll soon get the truth if they give John a ring
"Now tell me Mr Blewett", the announcer man do say
"Is it true what we've been told about the price of hay?
What's your opinion? What do you think of that?"
And John knows all the answers. He brings them out just pat!

Well Farmer John's some good to we, he's opened up his yard
So we could have an 'evening', and they all worked some hard
They cleaned out all the houses and laid down lots of hay
They started after milking and carried on all day
It can't be any easy job to make it all so neat
You wouldn't know that they had cows they made it smell so sweet

Then we went down with all the stuff that we had brought to sell
We had some 'andsome cake and things and cups of tea as well
Right back in the corner there was a cider vat
But that was all a bit hush hush, so we don't talk 'bout that
It all went on for hours and hours, with wagon rides and shows
There was raffles, games and wrassling and what else goodness knows

The choir all sang, the bandsmen played, they made the rafters ring
You could tell the boys was Cornish, the way that they could sing
Viscount and Lady Falmouth came up all that way
To open up the evening, and we didn't have to pay

Sir Alan and Lady Dalton, I saw that they was there
So you can see my 'ansome, 'twas some grand affair
They sat and had their pasties, saffron cake and tea

And didn't have no knifes nor forks, they ate it just like we
They sat around on bales of straw, and had a bit of chat
Then off they went round all the stalls, we thought a lot of that

They didn't give themselves no airs, they mixed with all the crowd
Once I thought they smiled at me, and that made me some proud
Then when the show was over, and they had gone away
We all agreed they'd been some nice and really made our day
And as for Farmer Blewett, his wife and children too
We couldn't thank them all enough for such a splendid do!
For all the time and money and energy they'd spent
But I still wish they would tell me where all that cider went!!!

Bessie and Mary

Bessie and Mary were sisters and neither had ever been wed
But they seemed content with each other, and the kind of life they had led
They lived far out in the country, in a cottage across a long lane
Where blackberries grew in the summer, and the fields were golden with
grain
You opened a gate into meadows, and there at the end of the track
Stood their little grey house with small window panes, and smoke drifting
up from the stack
They had a brown cow for their milk and their cream, and chickens that ran
round the floor
Round and round the kitchen they'd go, 'till Bessie showed them the door!

Bessie was buxom and bossy, with a no nonsense kind of an air
With a wrap-around pinney and black-wellied feet, and a tammy on top of
her hair
No one dreamed of tangling with Bessie, for our Bess called a shovel a
spade
All day long she bristled and bustled, buns to bake and cream to be made!
She was housewife and farmer and all things in between
The farm was her Kingdom, and Bessie was Queen
But Bess had a heart as big as the world, with plenty of room there for me
So she'd let me help her to brew and to bake, until it was time for tea

Mary was blind, from her birth I believe, but to Mary that caused no great
pain
For what Mary wanted to do then that's what Mary did, over and over
again
She could kindle the fire with one flick of a match, milk the cow straight
into a pail
It never came into her reckoning at all, that one day she might possibly fail!

As a small child I would stare in her face, not believing her eyes couldn't
see
For whenever I met her, before I could speak, she would call out my name
to me
With her tap-tapping stick she travelled along, no fast cars to be feared in
her day
Tall and impressive, like a ship in full sail, she went on her confident way

When still very young, I was taken away, and never saw the sisters again
And as children do, I soon found other friends and forgot the farm and the
lane
But as I grew older my mind wandered back, and I wanted to find them
again
Mary and Bessie must long have passed on, but surely some trace would
remain?
And so I went back to the place of my birth, and there on the top of the hill
In the small village churchyard, surrounded by trees, I found them –
together still
And together still they'll be waiting with Heaven's gate opened wide
"Now wipe your shoes" says Bessie "before you come inside"

When the Children Come to Stay

Granny, let's go walking up upon the moors
Don't you think it's far too nice to stay shut up indoors?
We can do some yomping, pretend we're Para Two
We'll hide away behind some rocks, then jump out at you
Perhaps we'll take some sandwiches, and have a fizzy drink
We can take our backpacks, Granny, wadya think?

Granny, let's go swimming, I've brought my trunks with me
Oh! Don't be silly, Granny, it's as easy as can be!
You don't have to worry, we'll take good care of you
Oh! Granny you look funny! Your toes are turning blue!
Perhaps you need a cup of tea, and we could have a bun
Oh! Isn't this exciting! Aren't we having fun?

Can we do some baking? Oh! Gran you promised me!
I won't be any trouble, just you wait and see!
I won't get flour upon the floor, I'll do it just like you
Can I have some currants please, just a tiny few?
We can make enormous lots, and pile them high as me
Shall we have a picnic then, and eat them all for tea?

Granny I feel very tired, I think I'll go to bed
Hang on that looks exciting, I'll watch TV instead!
Yes please I'd like a biscuit and a glass of orange juice
Granny! Looks what's happening, my tooth is working loose
No Granny, I'm not sleepy, and look it's still quite light
All right then, where's my teddy bear? I love you Gran, goodnight

The Price of Fish

Today the harbour is quiet, no boats have sailed from the quay
It looks like a storm may be brewing, and the wind howls in from the sea
We sit and quietly chatter of friends we have known and lost
And we laugh and boast of big catches, while inwardly counting the cost
For the sea that gives us our living, providing for children and wives
Demands a terrible penance, that for fish men shall pay with their lives

Sometimes at night, in the lash of a storm, I hate the demands of the sea
But when once more I stand safe on shore, I feel the tides tugging at me
In the teeth of a gale, when cold fear grips my heart, I vow I will do this no
more
But for people like me there's no life but the sea, so I'll still take my
chance as before
For though I may love it, or though I may hate it, this calling has passed
down to me
And, like father, like brother, I know no other, my life or my death is the
sea

My Christmas Day

Yes, my dear, I would believe
That it's already Christmas Eve
I'm just home from Christmas shopping
Legs are aching, eyelids dropping
Children squabbling, painful head
I think I'll spend all day in bed!
Oh! How happy I would be
If I were you, and you were me
Now it's nearly Christmas Day

On the hill, the church bells call
"Peace on earth, goodwill to all"
My goodwill's been in short supply
And 'peace on earth' just passed me by
But – we sing songs of hope and joy
To celebrate a baby boy
Then it's so very plain to me
There's nowhere else I'd rather be
To welcome Christmas Day

Christmas cake and hot mince pies
Shining joy in children's eyes
The young ones coming home to stay
To share with Mum and Dad this day
Gran with baby on her knee
Singing carols by the tree
I smile at you, you smile at me
And there's nowhere else I'd rather be
Than home for Christmas Day

A Poem for Christmas

"Write me a poem for Christmas"
That's what the Reverend said
So I sat down quietly waiting
'Till these thoughts came into my head

I thought of the fun times at Christmas
Of warm fires and soft candlelight
Then I remembered the wandering shepherds
And the star in the cold eastern night

I thought of the feasting and carols
And presents piled high round the tree
Then of three wise men on a journey
In search of a promised baby

I remember the birth of my own son
With the joy he has brought our way
And I think I might know how Mary felt
On that very first Christmas Day

So let's treasure this Christmas feeling
The love and the happiness
And all try to care for each other
Happy Christmas to all and God bless

The Church on the Hill (St Denys)

The church on the hill, how proudly it stands
As it watches the houses below
And beckons the people to come to its arms
As their forefathers did long ago

It comforts the mourners who cry in their grief
And watches with sadness their sorrow
Then whispers "Hold fast and be strong
There will be a better tomorrow"

Its bells peal with joy as they welcome a bride
As they've welcomed so many before
Then she and her groom make their vows before God
And Mother Church is smiling once more

Tenderly, gently, the baby it cradles
When it's brought to its Baptism Day
With infinite tenderness welcomes the child
"Come join us" the church seems to say

The Church on the hill, how proudly it stands
As it watches the houses below
And welcomes the people, who come to it still
As their forefathers did long ago

The Brixham Boys

The Brixham Boys went visiting on a summer holiday
They packed their best pyjamas, and started on their way
They headed straight for Cornwall, without a backward glance
To have a great adventure – given half a chance!
They reached their destination, at Granny's B&B
Where service wasn't all that great, but at least the food was free!

The Brixham Boys loved footballing and couldn't wait to play
They got their Grandad joining in – he couldn't walk next day!
They practiced taking penalties – I hope you're listening Glen
When England's next in trouble, these could be your men
They used tins of beans for goalposts, it made good sense to me
For when the game was over they had goalposts for their tea

Godzilla kept on calling those macho Brixham Boys
So off they went to monster land, amid the heat and noise
They thought the film was marvellous, Godzilla was a dear
'Twas only poor old Granny sat quivering with fear
They treated her most kindly, and said it was OK
It didn't really matter, she'd be grown up one day

The Brixham Boys had lots of fun on their summer holiday
But one day they started thinking, and their thinking went this way
We miss our Mum and we miss our Dad, and we miss our sister too
We miss our home and we miss our pets, so they knew just what to do
They packed their best pyjamas and started on their way
And headed straight for Devon, and Brixham, in the Bay

Granny's Doing Fine

How hard to be a wrinkly crone
Bowed of back, and gnarled of bone
Where once was taut and rosy skin
Now resides a double chin

The eyes that late were bright and clear
Have got a tendency to blear
And hair that once was thick and fair
Oh! What a sad disaster there!

Her neck is in a shocking state
Tried Oil of Ulay – just too late!
Perhaps she should take in the slack
And tuck it neatly round the back

You'd think her skinny legs will break
How much more can the poor things take?
But don't feel sorry for old Granny
She's the one who's cute and canny

She may look old to you and me
But she's as happy as can be
Inside she feels like twenty-one
Granny's having lots of fun

From Us to You with Love

on our 30th anniversary of St Dennis CRC
(now Cancer Research UK)

Now gather round, my children, and listen to my tales
Of walks and talks, and knit ins, and giant jumble sales
It all began so long ago, in nineteen sixty-two
When you were all so very young, and we much younger too
It doesn't seem so long ago, that Ralph with his small clan
Thundered into action, and the mighty fight began
Of course, our eyes were brighter then, our skins were wrinkle free
But we're still in here fighting, we are St Dennis CRC

It started very slowly, with just a chosen few
Then the rest of us were netted, and like Topsy it just grew
With sponsored walks and harvest homes, you should have heard us sing!
"We plough the fields and scatter" – we made the rafters ring!
And then we had the knit-in, 'twas fine for all the girls
But Oh! Our poor wee laddies didn't know their plain knit from their purls
The carnival brought hippies, now just who can they be?
Yes, that's right, you've got it, St Dennis CRC

We've held a million raffles, well, give or take a few
We've brewed and baked, until we ached, and sold it all to you
Our jumble sales are famous for bargains, biscuits, tea
But never drop your brolly or it's 'Bargain 20p'
So we've laughed and cried through thirty years, made lots of money too
But always we remember, we owe it all to you
To all our firm and faithful friends, and others soon to be
Our heartfelt thanks, to one and all, from St Dennis CRC

Growing Old (dis)Gracefully

Now I'm seventy, I'll be an old lady
Act with genteelness and grace
Sit with a hand-knitted rug round my knees
And a benevolent smile on my face
Now I've got to my three score and ten years
I'll give up my wild, girlish ways
I'll sit in an armchair and bore all the kids
With my stories of long ago days
I'll be the soul of decorum
And impress with my delicate charm
When crossing the road I'll ask a Boy Scout
"Will you kindly just lend me your arm?"
I'll do all the things that old ladies should
Like sit in the corner and knit
While drinking my tea from a fine china cup
Sip by elegant sip

But that does sound incredibly boring
I think I shall need some more time
To get used to this change in my lifestyle
To rush things would be such a crime!
So I'll shorten my skirts just a little
Perhaps just a glimpse of the knee?
The legs are looking in reasonable shape
Oh yes, that really is me!
A little touch of pink blusher?
That's right back in fashion I hear
I think rosy cheeks are so flattering, don't you?
Oh, I'm so glad you think so my dear!

I really feel quite a spring chicken again
And the old boys are becoming quite matey
So I'll throw over the traces, and kick up my heels
And postpone being old till I'm eighty!

Pollution

"Pollution?" said the chairman of the meeting
"Is undoubtedly a national disgrace
You'd think that people really would know better"
And he puffed his cigar smoke into my face

"Pollution?" said the captain of the tanker
"Is a constant source of grief and pain to me
I cannot think why people are so thoughtless"
And he opened wide his bilges to the sea

"Pollution?" said the owner of the factory
As he watched his chimneys belch into the sky
"I really wish I could afford to stop it"
And he walked towards his Bentley with a sigh

"Pollution?" said the pusher of the hard drugs
"Pollution of the body is a sin"
And he held his hand out ready for the money
As he watched the junkie push the needle in

The Poor Old Girl

Who is that wrinkly woman standing on the stair
She really should be careful standing over there
She must be really elderly with hair that is so grey
Do you suppose her bosom always drooped that way

Her bottom is extremely fat, her waist has thickened too
It must be quite a heartache to have veins that are so blue
Her forehead is so furrowed it really is a sin
She should pull out that whisker that's sprouting from her chin

If I'm not much mistaken her neck is 'going' too
She ought to wear a chiffon scarf, that's what the film stars do!
I wonder why she's staring? Whoever can she be?
Oh! Dear! That 'wall's' a mirror, the poor old girl is me!

Ready – Steady – Oops!

Why can't I make a pasty that looks the same each time
Like all the bakers' pasties do, on the production line?
I've had fifty years of practice, that should have taught me how
Seven thousand pasties, I should have learned by now!

I make the perfect pasty, when it's just 'him' and me
With crimping that's *par excellence* and perfect symmetry
The hole's right in the middle and not a single tear
Oh yes, I'm Mrs Beaton when no-one else is there

So why, when we've got visitors and I'm anxious to impress
Do all the bloomin' pasties turn out to be a mess?
The pastry's like lace curtains, with patches like a quilt
And brown bits on the bottom where all the gravy's spilt

But still, when all is said and done, and the thing is on your plate
It's the taste that really matters, and the 'teddies' and the 'mate'
I'll never be an Ainsley, the TV invite will not come
But who needs fame and fortune when the pasty's in your tum?

!!! Totally Eclipsed !!!

We're full of wild excitement now the great eclipse is here
And we're all ready for it – well almost, pretty near!
We know that countless millions are coming here to stay
Unless they all get frightened off, and think they'll stay away
Every bed is booked in Cornwall, they told us long ago –
Except for all those vacancies, the ones they didn't know!

The roads may well be grid locked from Plymouth to Penzance
So we'll call in all the constables, not leave a thing to chance
We'll all have our appendix out, perhaps our tonsils too
And get a set of dentures made, in case we can't get through
We're stocking up on toilet rolls, it seems the thing to do
I wonder if I'd have much luck renting out our loo?

We want to share, dear millions, our full eclipse with you
Don't let the media scare you, we know just what to do
Perhaps 'twill be more sensible to split this thing in half
We're pretty smart, we Cornish, so don't you think we're daft
We'll contact all the visitors and tell them not to fear
Half of them come this time, then, have another one next year!

A Big Mis-Steak

She was a post-war blushing bride when rationing was rife
Just newly struggled from her teens, she strove to be a wife
No brasses ever shone so bright, no black-lead stove more gleamed
Oh, she would be a perfect wife – or so she fondly dreamed
She would be faithful until death, in harmony they'd dwell
No secrets she would have from him, no lies she'd ever tell

And so a week or two passed by, in perfect wedded bliss
Each morn was greeted with a smile, each night time with a kiss
Then off went hubby to his work, a proud and happy man
While little wifey, playing houses, their meal began to plan
Ration books still neat and shiny, off she went to buy some meat
"Bit of beef dear" said the butcher, "that's your lot until next week!"
What to make the wifey wondered, planning is the golden rule
She put the meat, (perhaps unwisely) on the window ledge to cool

Off she went in gay abandon, thinking now of this and that
But never for a single moment, of next doors scheming, thieving cat
Puss cat, thinking he's in heaven, steak clutched firmly in his teeth
Makes a beeline for the garden, and the dirty earth beneath
Out the window our bride follows, after him in hot pursuit
Wailing like a tortured banshee, using words like catch and shoot
Meat successfully recovered, still intact but worse for wear
Our heroine sits, worries, wonders, can she, will she? Does she dare?

Some hours later at the table, husband fondly smiles at wife
Thinks how lucky to have found her, as he picks up fork and knife
Thank you darling for my dinner, do have some, it's quite sublime
No! I'd rather watch you eat it, the pleasure darling is all mine
And so she watches rapt and spellbound, as he tucks into the meat
And prays that she might be forgiven for her first, well meant deceit.

Fat Fights Back

Why can't I be fat if I want to?
Why do I have to be slim?
Who first decreed I be thin as a reed?
Who said to be plump is a sin?

I want to be fat and voluptuous
Dress up in the sassiest gear
Who first "predicted" my girth be restricted?
I can't see myself from the rear!

I don't want to be a top model
The catwalk holds no charms for me
If they think being dumpy makes me look frumpy
Then that's how it's going to be!

Let them spend their days counting calories
I'm giving all diets a miss
I'll stay curvy and happy, full-faced and zappy
Oh! Eating this chocolate is bliss!

Hendra Ghosts

I sit on the Downs at Hendra, just a buzzard for company
Alone in the gorse and the heather, I dream of how things used to be
I see old men tramping the pathways, in the wind, the cold and the rain
To dig, to hew, and to lowster, then turn round and trudge home again

I see them in cloth caps and worn jackets, with trousers tied at the knee
Clinging like flies to the clay face, is that really how things used to be?
I see their flickering lanterns as they work in the dark of the night
Wielding their picks and their shovels, and praying for first morning light

I think I can hear ghostly voices, quietly singing a hymn
And I envy these men of religion, with faith that nothing could dim
I hear the echoing laughter, as a joke is shared with a friend
For these were men of good humour, of courage without any end

I see dim lights in the windows, candles to lighten their way
To homes, to wives and to children, to warmth at the end of the day
I watch them asleep in the firelight, the oil lamps hanging above
Men who were poor in possessions, but men who were wealthy in love

How I wish I could peer through the windows of time, to see them at work
and at play
To live as they lived, to see what they saw, to feel as they felt, for one day
But, wish as I may, I can never recapture how things used to be
So we'll just sit here at peace together, the buzzard, the ghosts and me

A Whitemoor Boy

in memory of Ray Neal 1902 – 1999

Ray Neal was a Whitemoor boy, Whitemoor to the core
A son of rock and heather, of gorse, and clay, and moor
He told how, when he was a child, his father prayed and then
The children, in a circle, would softly say "Amen"

So Ray grew up, became a man, and always he was sure
That when at last the time should come, he'd land at God's front door
His place in heaven was waiting, of that he had no doubt
It was just the when and where, and how, he wasn't sure about

Then he saw his Maker waiting, stepped through the open door
And said "I'm here at last dear Lord, my earthly life is o'er
"It wasn't always easy Lord, I'm sure you know that's true
"I met some rocky patches along my road to you

"I've been a long time coming, but I hope that you don't mind
"You know how hard it is Lord, to leave your friends behind
"But everything's alright now, Lord", and he looked round heaven with joy
And thought how much like home it felt, to a true born Whitemoor boy

The Bee's Knees or Holy Moses!

There are many ways of serving God
I'm sure you will agree
Some are universal
Some just for you and me

One way I'm sure would please Him
To help your fellow man
Perhaps to brighten up the life
Of some deserving Gran

But even He must be surprised
When looking down below
To see the special lengths to which
His Reverend son will go

What greater sacrifice be made?
What greater wish to please?
Than for your local minister
To flash his hairy knees?

But, if all His works are wonderful
Which cannot be denied
Then your legs are no exception
So wear those shorts with pride!

Our Golden Years

Dedicated to Mary and Percy

I look across the room at you
Contented in your chair
No need for us to speak or touch
Enough that you are there
Beside me as you've always been
For fifty loving years
Years of making memories
Shared laughter and shared tears

Those early, tender, loving years
The world just you and me
Then, in the twinkling of an eye
We were a family
What joy our children brought us
I know they always will
What fun they brought into our lives
And how we love them still

Now it's our golden wedding day
The church bells start to ring
Sweet memories flood into my mind
My heart begins to sing
It sings for happy times we've had
And others still to be
For years now gone, and years to come
The love you've shared with me

If I could choose throughout the earth
The world be mine to view
I would not change a single thing
My love I'd still choose you

Dear Friend

Dear friend, I write to thank you for having me to tea
The cake and conversation, your hospitality
The time passed very quickly, and I was sad to go
But soon it would be morning, I needed sleep and so
Remembering your company, as ever a delight
I nestled on my pillows to spend a restful night

BUT –

I found myself at Aintree, a pretty sight to see
Forty mighty stallions, and on a donkey, me!!
Round and round the course we went, took Beechers in our stride
"It's easy girl" the jockey said "just put one foot each side"
"I think it would be helpful dear" I heard one rider say
"If you and your little donkey could both face the same way!"

AND –

I sailed upon a mighty ship – I'd always wanted to
I was the toast of one and all, both passengers and crew
The captain walked me round the deck, it almost turned my head
Then I saw the prettiest iceberg shining straight ahead
Something stirred inside my brain, I tried hard not to panic
Then I looked down upon her side, read HMS Titanic

THEN –

I joined the village carnival, perched proudly on my steed
Dressed totally in character, of clothes I had no need
The crowd turned up in thousands to see the big parade
And I felt quite elated at the impression I had made

Everyone was laughing which didn't seem quite fair
But then I started blushing, Godiva had ***long*** hair

SO –

Dear friend, I write to thank you for having me to tea
The cake and conversation, your hospitality
But may I ask you kindly, don't be offended please
When next you ask me for a meal, ***go lightly on the cheese***

'Her' or Me?

I'm trying to take myself in hand
And act like a sensible girl
But though my body is ready and willing
My head's in a feverish whirl
I've tried to be prompt with the dinner
But it seems such a hard thing to do
The knives and forks are all ready
But it's my head that remains in a stew

I do my best to meet every deadline
My planning is bang up to date
Then my brain spots a thrilling adventure
And doesn't come back 'till too late
I am the most fabulous 'starter'
I've "cardis" and jumpers galore
Well I've five sleeves, two fronts, and a couple of backs
The rest of the wool's in the drawer

Now we come to the crux of the matter
The dilemma is plain as can be
If this fabulous woman takes over
What will happen to scatter-brained me?
So I'm putting the vote to the public
Just to put my poor brain at its ease
Shall I let her take over, or give her the boot?
All answers on plain postcards please

Now this is my present dilemma
When I think of my very last ride
I have visions of me still on journey
While you are all waiting inside

So when you are wishing me God speed
No flowers please of pink or of red
Just think how much 'heaven time' I'm missing
And bring an alarm clock instead!

An Old Woman's Lament

Has anyone found my memory?
I had it yesterday
Now it's disappeared again
It just won't seem to stay

I have it in the morning
It's gone again by tea
Just when I think it's coming back
It waves goodbye to me

I know exactly what I want
I know it's up the stair
But by the time I've reached the top
I wonder why I'm there

I think I will go shopping
I'd better write it down
Oh dear the list is still at home
While I'm stuck here in town

Never mind, I'll busk it
It shouldn't be too bad
Now get yourself together girl
What was on that pad?

I'm sure that it was sugar
Perhaps it could be tea
If I sit here and think awhile
It's sure to come to me

Oh well I've bought some super shoes
So I'd better catch the train
Oh Lord, I'm just two stops from home
And I've left the car again!

Well Suited

I'm going to a wedding – it's quite a grand affair
With all the local gentry expected to be there
Of course I did some planning, I started months ago
Got all my gear together, and now it's time to go
I went to a couturier, 'cos I needed something smart
Though when I saw the prices it wreaked havoc with my heart!
But I'd gone along that road too far to give in now and stop
Besides I'd seen the perfect thing, just inside the shop

The skirt was long and slender, but my tummy looked quite flat
And I looked in all the mirrors, said, "Does my bum look big in that?"
The answer was a negative, with which I must agree
The suit that's in the wardrobe looks like 'twas made for me
I've gone and got a super hat, but isn't this a caper?
The label says: "Don't wear in rain", this hat is made of paper!
I've bought myself a posh corsage, a buttonhole won't do
And I've got a really perfect match to bag and hat and shoe

I'm getting quite excited, 'twill be a triumph just you see
Those very smart accessories and the suit just made for me
And now I'm getting ready, I'll just don my suit and then…
Hey! This suit, I know was size fourteen, now it's shrunk to ten!

Yours sincerely

"I really love your county" the politician said
"Have done since I was small
It really is my favourite place
The finest of them all

I take the greatest interest
In everything you do
And all my time is focused now
On what is best for you

I understand your problems
That go with this terrain
They're endemic to the region
But we'll put them right again

Now sadly I must leave you
These ten minutes have flown by"
Then turning to his trusty aide
"Where the – (bleep) – am I?"

This character is entirely fictitious, and bears no resemblance whatsoever
to any politician known to the author

Sensual Perception

Oh, lucky me, that I can see the gorse upon the hill
Fold on fold, a cloth of gold, where I can take my fill
Can stroke the granite boulders as I am strolling by
And watch the lonely minestacks point fingers to the sky

Oh, lucky me, that I can lie upon the rugged heath
A mackerel sky above me, a bracken bed beneath
Where I can hear the seagull's cries upon the morning air
By roaring sea that calls to me, come fight me if you dare

Oh, lucky, me that I can smell the scents of sea and moor
Sweet honey-scented heather, sharp seaweed on the shore
The taste of salt upon my lips as I look out to sea
The sea that takes you from my arms, please bring you back to me

Oh, lucky me that I can say "Come friend and with me stand
Till we have filled our senses with this, beloved land"

Daffodil Days

Wherever we wander, wherever we go
Our senses are quickened, our hearts are aglow
The sun may not shine, and the rain it may teem
But the world is alight with the daffodil's gleam

In hedgerows and gardens, with trumpets held high
They raise their bright faces to smile at the sky
With reckless abandon and hearts full of glee
They wave and they beckon to all that they see

And out in the woodlands, beneath nodding trees
A carpet of gold does a dance in the breeze
As gaily they wander o'er meadow and lea
Ahead of us stretches this vast yellow sea

In fields and on hillsides, for mile upon mile
They glow and they glisten, they dance and they smile
Away to the world's end, a shimmering haze
Oh, these joyous, heaven-sent 'Daffodil Days'

Queen Katie

Once I owned a little cat
The sweetest cat you ever did see
A skinny cat, a scaredy cat
But that little cat belonged to me

I could have had a kitten –
There were plenty there to see
But Kate peeped out from her rescue cage
So I brought her home with me

And now I had a little cat
Not the best of buys, you'll see
Eight years old and short of teeth
But that little cat belonged with me

Two years have passed since Katie came
And we live compatibly
She kindly lets me stay with her –
As long as she's Queen Bee!

So now I have a little cat
The sweetest cat you ever did see
Who rules the roost and makes it known
"That little human belongs to me"

The Widow's Mite

She counted the pennies in her hand and wished that it was more
She'd seen five pound notes and ten pound notes, and silver coins galore
As people opened their wallets to see what they could spare
And her eyes grew round with wonder to see how much was there

Then she peered at the label on the tin; what was that it said?
'For the hungry and the homeless' the little lady read
She thought of her neat and cosy home where she could close the door
And she wasn't hungry was she, so how could she be poor?

She crossed the road with her old lady walk, and smiled at the man with the
tin
As she lifted her hand with its tiny hoard and carefully dropped it in
Then she put her empty drawstring purse back in her empty bag
And smiled a small contented smile, for she'd given all she had

And the Gods smiled on her kindly, for though her gift seemed small
Sometimes what seems the smallest gift is the greatest gift of all

The Ballad of Billy Bray, the Dancing Preacher

Did you 'ear the tale of Billy Bray, a Cornish boy from Twelveheads way?
Though Billy's family was poor, they was honest; Wesleyan to the core
But Bill, when 'ee was still a lad, went off the rails and turned to bad
If all the tales they told was true, he liked 'smut' and drink – fast women
too!

"Ee went on this way to twenty nine; till one day, workin' in the mine
The rocks above 'is head gave way; and Billy quickly learned to pray!
He fell upon his knees and said "Wot 'appened there? I should be dead!
I'll never take a drink agen I'd 'ave gone to hell if I'd died then!"

So Billy, now a much-changed man, became a part of God's rich plan
Up and down the roads he pranced; he laughed and prayed, he sang and
danced
And stopped each passing man and maid "How long since you last knelt
and prayed?"
He shouted out "The Lord be praised!" 'til 'ee nearly drove the neighbours
mazed.

Then came the time for 'im to go: 'ee had no fear of death, and so
Billy couldn't wait to die and "join my Father in the sky"
He shouted "Glory, glory be, it's Heaven and Paradise for me!"

*Billy died on May 28th 1868, having, if local legend is to be believed,
'danced his way to Heaven'.*

The Pity of it All

She sat alone in her lonely room, wondering how they were
The ones who'd promised her company, who said that they'd be there
She remembered the days of long ago, when she'd been one of a pair
How they'd laughed and joked with all their friends; what times they'd had
to share

Then the one she loved had had to go and she was left alone
But the friends all did their very best and called her on the phone
But as the days and weeks went by and their lives stayed in twos
Seeing her reminded them of what they had to lose

They felt guilty at their happiness, of the love they still could share
But they told her "Do come round one day": to ring, and they'd be there
She tried to call them, many times: she sat and held the phone
But couldn't find the courage to turn up all alone

So, she sat alone in her lonely room, wondering how they were
The ones who'd promised her company, who'd said that they'd be there
And they sat and wondered how she was, and why she didn't call
While we can only sit and think "Oh, the pity of it all"

The Re-Generation Game

When I was ten the world was my oyster
Life was forever, and time had stood still
Each day was a lifetime spread out for my pleasure
To use as I wanted – my lifetime to fill
But that was back then – when I was ten

When I was twenty, my world still kept spinning
The years spread before me, no end yet in sight
Life was for living, the candle for burning
The flame shining brightly, by day and by night
There was still time a-plenty, when I was twenty

I passed thirty, then forty, without seeing them go
I'd got me a husband, we'd got us a son
Each day brought us joy, a memory to treasure
But how quickly they sped, gone before they'd begun
Still, forty was fun, with a husband and son

Fifty, sixty, then seventy; now eighty is looming
And time's going faster than ever before
The bones they are creaking, the hair is retreating
No Botox can banish the wrinkles galore
And I've really got weighty, now I am eighty

So I'm going away for re-cycling
And starting all over again
I'll be coming back rockin' and rollin'
Now I'm reverting to ten

Oh Yeah!

The Empty Nester

"My nest is empty," the lady said
"My little fledgling has flown
I didn't notice how time had gone by
Didn't see how my baby had grown"

"How shall I manage without him?
How fill all the days that are left?
I thought I would have him for ever
Now he's left me alone and bereft"

"I've looked in his room, no more dirty socks
No rubbish all over the floor
There'll be no more phoning at midnight
'Cos he can't find his key to the door"

"My nest is empty", the lady said
Now, what will my future be?
I'll soak in the bath, paint my nails, that's what
And spend all my time spoiling ME!"

Yippee!

God's Cheerleader

"It's quiet today for a Thursday"
God thought, as he sat on His throne
Then Peter approached in a tizzy
"Dear God, see who's coming – it's Joan!"

"Oh good" said the Lord, broadly smiling
"I'm glad that she answered my call
She wasn't too keen and she argued a bit –
Said how much she's be missed by them all"

"Now with that I just couldn't argue
She's the apple of everyone's eye
But I've known for a while Heaven needed her smile
And their memories will help **them** get by"

"Well, I wasn't waiting for that one!"
Joan said, with a bit of a grin
"But now that I'm here I can see lots to do
Come on Peter, it's time to begin!"

By midday all the angels were smiling
By teatime she'd started a choir
To go with the singing, she'd started bell-ringing
But poor Peter had started to tire!

Now the Heavens are rocking with laughter
It's Joan's cheeky poems again!
So, though we may grieve, we still have to believe
Our loss is Heaven's great gain.

In memory of Joan, my sister

The Voice of an Unborn Child

I am a child as yet unborn
I have no voice, no vote, no choice
The life I'll live is the one you give
Please think of me

I may be your grandchild, nephew, son
A part of you, just now begun
Give me the chance to see the sky
And watch the billowing clouds roll by
Please think of me

I wish to live a life like you
Fresh air to breathe; good things to do
I want to live a normal span
Grow up and be an honest man
Please think of me

Some say the risks are very small
For my sake, take no risks at all
Don't take the chance that I may die
Don't watch my parents mourn and cry
Please think of me

I am a child as yet unborn
I have no voice, no vote, no choice
The life I'll live is the one you give
PLEASE think of me

Written in response to the on-going threat of a mass incinerator in St Dennis, Cornwall

Hurrah for Coffee Mornings

Once a month, on Tuesday, we have a coffee time,
That should be coffee morning, but I couldn't find a rhyme!
It's well known in the village, folks come from far and near
To look at all our bargains, and take a cup of cheer
They sit around the tables and have a bit of chat
A little harmless gossip, we all like some of that

We have skirts and coats and jumpers, shoes laid out in rows
Saucepans, toast racks, pot plants, goodness only knows
We really never know ourselves until the very day
What treasures we shall offer and they will take away
Sometimes we get a single shoe, or a 'pair', one six, one four
Or a 'Dolly Parton' brassiere, that carries all before!
We get some gorgeous jumpers, just right for lovely lasses –
And then the slightly strange one, made when Granny lost her glasses
Now the underwear is interesting – some sexy as can be –
Some in cotton interlock, held fast at waist and knee

Then a lady spots a winter coat, she's not all that impressed
"Oh well, I 'spose it's not *that* bad, 'twill mix in with the rest"
But as she offers fifty pence I beg her "Let it be,
Madam, that's my Sunday best – that coat belongs to me!"

A Prayer Unspoken

"I do not pray", she said,
"To whom would I pray?
And what should I say?
I do not pray" she said

Then she heard a child cry –
"God, oh my God, why
Must that small child die?"
When she heard a child cry

War came to the world –
"Oh please give us peace
Make all hatred cease
We need peace in our world"

Spring brought joy to the earth
Her heart sang to the sky –
"How lucky am I
God only knows why"

"I do not pray" she said
To whom would I pray
And what should I say?
I do not pray" she said

God listened, and smiled
"Oh, my child, my dear child"

The New Recruit

So you've got a new Angel in Heaven?
Well, he really is one of a kind
And there's one or two things that's worth knowing
So if you really won't mind –
Do you think we could make a suggestion
About heavenly choirs, and halos and things?
It just wouldn't suit him to sit on a cloud
And it's a definite no-no to wings!

He's never been much of a harp man
He's more of a 'do-er' you see
So if you could find him a mower
He'll be happy as happy can be –
With a nice patch of grass, his Elysian field
That he can keep neatly, tidied and mown
We shall picture him there, and we'll smile at the thought
And know he has safely reached home

For Mike, with love 2003

In Shades of Gold

God thought the world looked a little bit dingy
Lacking a smidgen of colour maybe?
Twas the season twixt Christmas and Easter
And people's spirits were as grey as the sea

He thought them a trifle ungrateful
What was wrong with the snowflakes so white?
But then the winter had seemed long and dreary
So perhaps the poor darlings were right!

He looked at the plants with a critical eye
End to end green, patches purple and pink
And thought on the whole He'd done a good job
Then "I know what's lacking, some yellow, I think"

So he fashioned a flower of most delicate hue
With pale creamy petals that gleamed in the light
And he smiled at the primrose as he sent it to earth
But wished it had been just a little more bright

So the daffodil followed to gladden folk's hearts
So strong and so tall, a remarkable fellow
With a trumpet that lifted its face to the heavens,
A trumpet of brightest, shining true yellow

"I'm getting the hang of this colouring thing"
God thought as he watched His next vision unfold
Take root and grow strong as it covered the land
With a beautiful carpet of pure burnished gold
"Now my mission's accomplished, let life take its course
No flower can compare with my beautiful gorse"

My Christmas List

We were talking together of Christmas
And how quickly it comes round each year
Of turkey and puddings and presents
And wasn't everything incredibly dear?
Wasn't it hard to know what to give folks?
So we decided we'd all write a list
That way everyone would be happy
And none of our friends would be missed

So I sat down in my comfy old armchair
And picked up my paper and pen
There must be dozens of things that I needed
Had wanted for ages – but then…
I found they had lost their importance
Now I know just what I must choose
Not so exciting as perfume or wine
But these things I really can use!

Understanding, compassion and caring
To replace what has drifted away
And to know what the other man's feeling
To walk in his shoes for one day
A little self-knowledge would be a good thing
Not too much, I can't handle a lot
Perhaps just enough to know when to speak
But most of all, know when to stop!
Then, last in my stocking
Right down in the toe
A small seed of hope
That I can watch grow and grow

Till it covers the world
With a forest of love
If we want it enough
We *can* make it so

And perhaps just a very, very small diamond?

Travelling Companions

**A sinner's eye view of the proposed covenant
between the Anglican and Methodist churches**

God sat in His armchair in Heaven
Surveying His people below
And thought how much He still loved them
But weren't they incredibly slow?

He had sent them one world and one people
And no matter what colour or creed
They were programmed to love one another
But how He wished they would get up some speed

He wondered what on earth was the problem
Why they needed a 'yours' and a 'mine'
So He fast-tracked a message from Heaven
To say 'ours' would suit Him just fine
after all
If a man's favourite tipple is coffee
While his friend has a liking for tea
They'll just look at the menu together
And choose something on which they agree

One person always travels by airline
Another one gets there by train
But they'll both reach the same destination
And be travelling together again

Then God saw a glimmer of daylight
When He heard His dear children decide
That on their joint pathway to Heaven
They'd walk hand in hand, side by side

So He sent a giant consignment of goodwill
Mixed with patience, in case of delay
For if He'd taken six days to completion
They'd never get there in a day!

People Watching

Oh Lord, my knees are aching
I've been walking far too long
I'll just sit down upon this bench
And watch the passing throng
Well now, that's feeling better
This corner's made for me
I'll just lift up my paper
Then see what I can see

Oh my, that is a funny man –
The one across the street
With balaclava, mitts and scarf
And flip-flops on his feet.
He's far too old for jogging pants –
Especially in pale blue
I'd never let him out like that
What is it coming to?

Ooh! Here comes Lady Bountiful
What do you think of that?
All high heels and cashmere coat
And a 'fifties' pill-box hat!?!
But I bet when all is said and done
If we could only see
She's after all the 'two for ones'
And 'half price' just like me

Well, I never, look at this!
Two maidens in their teens
With sequin tops and six inch skirts
And nothing in between

Well I don't care what fashion says
Or what's shown on the telly
You'll never catch <u>me</u> in the street
With a diamond in *my* belly!

My word, I'm feeling peckish
So I think it's time to go
Just one more peep above my 'Mail'
With half-closed eyes – like so
Well, some people take the biscuit!
How nosy can you be?
That woman in the anorak
I'll swear she's watching me!

Has she got nothing better to do!?!

Life Goes On

"Life has to go on" the lady says
And she smiles as she goes on her way
And the world smiles back at her cheery face
Glad she's better – that now she's OK

"Yes, I'm keeping incredibly busy
There's always a great deal to do
I'm to-ing and fro-ing from morning to night
Now, tell me, how's life serving you?"

"Yes, I've so many wonderful memories
To bring out when I'm feeling too sad
So life goes on and I must go with it
While I treasure the years that we had"

She closes the door of her too quiet house
Looks at the dear pictured face on the wall
Says "I've managed another day, my love,"
Only then does she let the tears fall

For Jenny Fouracres 2003 – A very special lady

Blessings

What a day to rejoice
And say with one voice
We wish you a lifetime of love
The sweet scent of flowers
And content, happy hours
We wish you a lifetime of love

May your hearts dance with laughter
And joy ever after
As we wish you a lifetime of love
Loving hands to caress you
And kind words to bless you
We wish you a lifetime of love

Caring friends without measure
Fond memories to treasure
We wish you a lifetime of love
God bless you and hold you
His arms gently fold you
And give you a lifetime of love

The Goldcrest

It was just an ordinary day
Nothing special, you might say
Just two old people, slowly walking
Hand in hand, and laughing, talking

Drinking in the country air
And finding deep contentment there
Then gently, rippling like a breeze
There came a movement in the trees

And with fluttering of tiny wing
Appeared the smallest, magic thing
They dared not speak, said not a word
Just stood and watched that joyous bird

As it flipped from tree to tree
That show-off bird "Just look at me!"
And look they did, and wondered why
They could not have the power to fly?

How eyes so small could clearly see?
Such fragile wings reach top of tree?
Can such a small heart really beat?
And oh, such tiny claws and feet

Its head is gold, I wonder why?
Do birds go to heaven when they die?
It dipped its small gold- crested head
In last salute, then swiftly fled

And on they went, hearts full of joy
The aged girl, her loving boy
It was just an ordinary day
Nothing special you might say
Except that, for a little while
They saw once more with the eyes of a child

Goodbye Forever

It's the end of the road for you and me
I've decided I've taken my fill
You've let me down for the very last time
No more shall I bend to your will

I thought at the start that we'd care for each other
But you've never stuck to the deal
You've sat in the corner from the very first day
Just waiting to get your next meal

I begged you "Stop smoking," I said it was bad
But my pleading was always in vain
Just when I thought you had listened at last
There you were, puffing again!

In the dark of the night, when I've needed you most
You've gone out, left me cold and alone
When I've left my warm bed to coax you, "Please stay"
All I've found is a heart of pure stone

Yet still I feel sad that our ways have to part
But I know you will never stop cheating
So be gone from my heart, you faithless coal fire
I've ordered the new central heating!

For Bet, with Love

When her friends remember Betty
What do you think they'll see?
I bet it'll be a great big smile
As warm as a smile can be

When her friends remember Betty
What do you think they'll hear?
A joke and a saucy chuckle
And they'll know that Betty's near

When her friends remember Betty
They'll be proud that they can say
"Yes, I was close to Betty
And I'm glad she passed my way"

When her friends remember Betty
What do you think they'll feel?
They'll feel the warmth of her, all around
Helping their bruised hearts heal

And though they cannot see her now
And are parted for a while
They'll always hold her memory close
And remember with a smile

See you later, Bet.
In memory of a dear Cancer Research colleague who left us too soon

Party Time

We feel a little smug tonight, the way that people do
When they've been told they're marvellous, and can't deny it's true!
Our organiser tells us we're the best he's ever seen
What a pity he's used the self-same line wherever he has been!

We've raised a lot of money since 1962
But this is not the royal 'we', this 'we' is us and you
We couldn't do it on our own, without our friends to buy
The things we pile upon our stalls, so that's the reason why

Alan's put his tie on, a sight that's seldom seen
You really have to earn that, if you know what I mean
It takes tremendous efforts to make him tie that knot
But if you want to know the secret, well, money helps a lot!

Just cross his palm with silver or a cheque marked CRC
And it's round his neck like lightning, so fast the eye can't see!
So now we're gathered here tonight to say our thanks to you
A very loyal band of friends, for all the things you do

Every one of you is special, each has played their part
To make this evening happen, so, let the party start!
Let's all have a hooley, let's all have some fun
And pat each other on the back and say how well we've done!

Tomorrow we'll be serious; we'll fight the fight again
Tomorrow we'll fight dragons until the beasts are slain
But tonight's the night to celebrate, so let's raise our glasses high
And drink a toast to all of us – and Alan, DO take off that tie!

The Halcyon Years

My halcyon years didn't last long. By my ninth birthday they were fading, and long before my tenth they had gone, but the memories are oh, so sweet, perhaps made more so by time?

My memories are not of gambolling lambs, or the first cry of the cuckoo, but of running to school along a grass verge, running, running, alone but not lonely. Did I ever walk? I remember the cowslip I found one morning in the middle of the verge. Proud, straight and solitary, it was my friend, and every day I stopped to speak to it. I don't recall being sad when it died. By then I had discovered the violets, and little girls are fickle.

I can still feel the coolness of the leaves as I parted them, searching for the small, sweet violets, and the joy and wonder of finding each tiny flower. To this day they have a special place in my heart, and one small bunch of violets will give me greater pleasure than the most exotic orchid.

My summers were always sunny. Memory forbids that there should ever have been a rainy day. The sun always shone and the birds always sang, and so it shall ever stay in my memory.

I had a sister then, three and a half years – and a lifetime – older than I. For ten years she was my carer and my jailer, my pleasure and my pain, and how I missed her when she went. She left in the summer with the halcyon years, but that was yet to come, and fear had no part in our lives.

We didn't have a mother, but that was normal for us, and we accepted the life we'd been given. It didn't seem so very different from our friends.

Each summer was a lifetime, and a lifetime was forever. There were blackberries to pick, kindling to gather, and 'Down Under' to explore. To get 'Down Under' we had to slide on our backs down a slippery slope beneath overhanging trees leading from the bottom of our garden into a magic, secret meadow. In all the summer days we spent 'Down Under' I can't recall ever seeing an animal or another person there. Just two small girls wearing daisy-chain necklaces and perfume made from rose petals, running free as the wind.

In our summer search for blackberries we trudged the seemingly endless country lanes, and foraged in the farmer's fields. It didn't occur to us that these were private property. The fields were there, and so were we, and we belonged together. The biggest, blackest, juiciest berries, the ones I coveted most, were always just out of reach, and so it was that one dreadful summer day the walking stick I had borrowed from Granny 'walked' never to be seen again, but Granny was forgiving. She saw my quivering conscience and knew that was punishment enough.

The kindling was gathered in the 'plantation'. 'Picking sticks' was the name of the game, and there were always masses of small, broken twigs just the right size for little hands to scoop up into brown paper carrier bags to light the old Cornish range. This was where we snuggled like little chickens on cold winter evenings. The range was burnished like ebony and the brass knobs shone like stars in the lamplight. When the sitting room grate was lit – mostly at weekends, and when the parson came to tea – we sat and toasted bread and our toes while watching 'pictures' in the fire.

When autumn came it was time to run to the top of the hill to see if the horse chestnut had started to drop its harvest. The road would be covered with prickly green balls, and the search began to find the partly opened ones and prise out the conkers. I can't remember ever doing anything with the conkers, the finding and collecting was reward enough.

Then, in the space of a few short months, all had changed. Everything and everyone dear to me had vanished from my life, and with them the halcyon years. My sweet natured sister, so different to me, had lost her life almost before it began, and I found myself alone in a world of strangers. Overnight I grew up, and was never again to run and play in fields and woods.

But nothing can ever take from me my precious memories, where I can still run free in the fields, smell sweet violets, and hear the birds sing just for me. I can trickle my hand in the stream, make lemonade from crystals in an earthenware pitcher, and be a child again: and all is well.

Clarice in Callestick

I hope Callestick hasn't changed too much. For the first six or seven years of my life it was the only world I knew, safe, secure; where nothing much happened and very little changed.

It was only a hamlet really, a Cornish 'Lark Rise I suppose, but it held everything I needed: freedom to wander at will, a welcome at every house, and everyone happy to indulge a small chatterbox girl. So much so that when I announced my third birthday to all and sundry, I was showered with pennies and even a new hankie; what a pity I was made to return them all!

There was a small village shop where one day I was sent to buy cooked ham. In those days ham was home-cooked, and surrounded by a (to me) delicious savoury jelly: so, "A quarter pound of ham please, Mrs Fowler, and can I have half of it in jelly, please?"

"I don't think your Granny would like that, do you? So here's a quarter of ham for her sandwiches and some jelly for you". I couldn't think why she was laughing.

Because our mother had died when I was just a toddler, and my sister not much older, the people of Callestick seemed to take us under their wings. We never knew who donated the baby dolls that were left for us the next Christmas at the little Post Office. My sister announced that her doll was to be named Maisie. When she pulled rank and wouldn't allow mine to be Maisie as well, which seemed perfectly logical to me, mine became, somewhat oddly, Geezie! I wonder what happened to Geezie?

As I said, nothing much happened in Callestick; except for a few weeks in August, when the Naylors came to the village on holiday. Holidays were an unknown concept to me. I'd never had one, and didn't know anyone else who had. This was the early nineteen thirties, so there probably were other holiday-makers in places like Perranporth and Newquay, but not in our sleepy little backwater.

Oh, the excitement when Mrs Naylor talked to me. To my eyes she was like visiting Royalty, AND she came from London! I did everything but curtsey.

Picking black, white and red currants in Mrs Coad's garden, making lemonade from crystals at the village 'chute', and everyone being my friend; of such little things are a small child's memories made.

Yes, I hope Callestick hasn't changed too much.

St Piran's Day

March 5th is a very significant day for the people of Cornwall. It marks the special day of St. Piran, patron saint of miners and of Cornwall (Kernow).

You may have seen in Cornwall the black and white St Piran's flag fluttering from public places and hotels. It is much in evidence, together with the black and gold Cornish tartan; the blue and white robes of Cornish Bards; and the richly embroidered standards of the many Old Cornwall Societies, during the March 5th pilgrimage across the sand dunes of Perranporth to the site of the old lost church.

It was on the beach at Perranporth that St. Piran is said to have landed, after floating across from Ireland on a millstone!

Billy Bray – from Hell Raiser to Heaven's Recruiting Agent

When wondering what to write this month, I remembered an old Cornish character from many years ago, when Cornwall was world famous for its mining industry. In fact, if you lived toward West Cornwall, probably mining and farm labouring were the only two occupations open to most men.

Alongside the hard-living, hard-drinking culture of most miners ran the strong Non-Conformist Wesleyan religion; the Wesley brothers having paid several visits to Cornwall. The Wesleyans were later followed by the Methodists.

Into this environment, in 1794, was born William Trewartha (Billy) Bray. Billy's parents were poor but very respectable, and strong in their religion. It must have been a great heartache for them when Billy decided to take the path of the hard drinkers: to quote one writer of the time "Being a drinker, a carouser and a teller of dirty stories." Oh dear!

However, this was all to change; and after surviving a mining disaster Billy became the Dancing Preacher. Though I doubt many Cornish people would now know Billy's story, my father's generation would still relate the tale of how he went on to build the world-famous Kerley Downs (Three Eyes) Chapel, so named because of its three windows. For many years services were held in the Chapel each year to celebrate Billy's birthday; and for all I know maybe still are!

Days with Dad

I didn't have that many days living with Dad; about nine and a half years all told, but they are still fresh in my mind. There are no great earth-shattering memories, just little things that make up a small child's life: like the day when my father was turning one end of the rope so that my sister Freda and I could skip, and was told by a passing neighbour that he would be better employed planting his (somewhat neglected) garden instead! We thought that was hilarious.

At that time we were living at Littlewater, a short distance from the village of Goonhavern, and it was there that I saw the Northern Lights. Had my father not taken us outside to see this wonderful sight – highly visible, with no street lights or houses around – I would probably still believe it wasn't possible in this country. Thanks, Dad, good memory.

Every Saturday night when he went to the cinema, Dad would buy us a Tiffin chocolate bar, which he gave to us on Sunday morning; and every single weekend the same thing happened. Freda, three and a half years older than me, would leave her unopened Tiffin in a prominent place – and wait. I was absolutely determined that I would not eat mine until she ate hers too, but always my longing got the better of me: Then, with much yum-yumming, she would eat hers. I'm still just as sadly lacking in willpower!

It was in the garden at Littlewater, in 1938, that I saw my first aeroplane. The sun was shining, the sky was blue, and the threatened war seemed far away; but Dad decided that if it did happen he would rather like to be a pilot. In the event, the Ministry of Defence thought that, as a Master Carpenter, he would be much more useful building minesweepers!

Many years later my husband and I would often drive past Littlewater on our way to Perranporth and it still had the power to tug at my heartstrings.

Transport Nineteen-Thirties Style

I can picture it so clearly still. A big black car with a little oval window in the back, and my mother looking back and waving to me as she was driven off to the hospital. It's my first memory of a car, but then, I was only a little over two and a half years old.

Shortly after, I met my first bus. It seemed very big to me, with two long seats where the passengers sat facing each other. There was definitely no roof visible when I saw it, but perhaps there was a roll-top in case of rain? I do hope so! I didn't actually get to ride on it, but proudly watching my father climb on board and sail away into the distance was almost as good as.

Normally my father went everywhere on his trusty push-bike; on dark evenings complete with smelly carbide lamp on the front. On work days he loaded it up with his carpenter's tool bag and pedalled off to earn an honest crust, but it was also his leisure vehicle, taking him to town on Saturday nights to visit the 'pictures'. He once even loaded eight-year-old me on to the cross bar and took me from where we lived at Goonhavern to the railway station at Truro. I don't know how far that was, just that it felt TOO far!

Incidentally, on that journey, from Truro to Penzance, I was put in 'the care of the guard', something that would not be allowed today. The guard was not happy with me sitting alone in the railway carriage and took me into the guard's van, where I passed the journey happily perched on a packing case; even more unthinkable.

However, to regress a few years; in the early thirties my father was acquainted with Donald Healey of the Healey motoring family who lived in Perranporth: and so it came about that one sunny Sunday, up to our front door rolled the latest, sporty three-wheeled, open-topped car; Donald and friend in the two front seats, while Dad clambered into the 'dickie' seat at the back, and off they roared, for all the world like three 'Mr Toads' taking to the open road. Well, men always would be boys!

Wartime Porkies

During World War Two people had to register with shopkeepers to get their somewhat meagre food rations. Once registered they were stuck with each other for the following year.

One old lady I knew found a way of cheating the system. The first year she registered with Butcher A, and had her rations in the usual way, but at the beginning of the second year, while promising the ration books to Butcher A she actually gave them to Butcher B.

For several weeks, each time Butcher A called she had an excuse; she "Couldn't find the books just at the moment" or "Someone had taken them out to the grocers". She'd be sure to let him have them next time, so he let the little apple-cheeked, white-haired old lady have her meat until he eventually realised he'd been 'had.'

There was a big doorstep row, but he couldn't do a thing. He'd broken the law by letting her have the meat without food coupons in the first place.

I believe she did this until she ran out of gullible butchers.

How to Become a Vegetarian

One day the old gent from whom we rented rooms when we were first married, came in, plonked a rabbit on the table and said "There's your dinner". I was used to eating rabbit of course; everybody did in the forties and fifties. Tom even used to come courting with a brace of rabbits on the handlebars of his bike; he was a shooting man then, another thing that was natural to the clay country at that time – many men shot for the pot.

Anyway, there was I with a fully clothed rabbit, and my landlord expecting to see a neatly nude creature in a pie. I was afraid of doing it, but even more afraid of his scorn if I didn't! No, I didn't try to pluck it, and really I made quite a good job of skinning it – even if it did take half the day – that was until I got to the head! I knew it had to be chopped off, but why would it keep looking at me? In the end I had to pull the fur up over its face so that it couldn't watch me and give one almighty whack with a sharp knife. The first and only time I skinned a rabbit. Oh, and I skipped dinner.

Poor but Proud – a Widow's Story

Tom's Granny was widowed very young; her husband dying of 'apoplexy' on his way home from work, leaving her with five young children to support. To eke out her 'Lloyd George' – the Widow's Pension – she became a washerwoman.

This must have been in the early part of the century when washing was a zinc bath, a bar of hard soap, and water from the stream. Water for washing clothes, dishes, scrubbing – known as 'coddling' water was all dipped from the stream. Granny had a friend, also a widow, who walked from St. Dennis every Monday morning to a house at the far end of Nanpean, did the week's washing, then walked home again, a round trip of five miles. She always stopped at Granny's cottage on the way to and from, for a cup of tea, a rest and a chat.

The cottage only had one kitchen/living room, but this was looked after with loving care. The dull wooden table top was reversed on Sundays to become a highly polished 'best' table; and no matter how hard the times there was always a joint on that day. There was only the 'stove', a Cornish range, for heating and cooking. When the day's work was finished the top of the stove could be partly opened to provide an open fire. Always two kettles would be kept 'singing' on the stove to provide constant hot water: one often enamel for drinking, the other usually cast-iron, for dish (and people) washing.

Next to the stove was the flour 'hutch', a big wooden container with a hinged lid where a large cloth bag of flour was tipped to keep dry. The cloth bag was then washed, cut into squares and hemmed for handkerchiefs. There too, was a shelf on which were stored big blocks of salt; these had to be chopped with a knife, then crushed to a powder for use. I still remember running my finger along my own widowed Granny's salt shelf and licking it – and being told that my "blood would all dry up". Not yet it hasn't, Granny!

Three brave widows. Let us salute them.

The "Tail" of a Pig

Granny Andrews kept two pigs in an outhouse at the end of the garden, quite common in those days, especially in wartime. One was sold, the other killed and eaten; a great help during food rationing. I think you had to give up some of your meat coupons, but by no means all.

My dreaded job was to collect pig swill from her friends and relatives in large lidless tins and carry it home through the village; in one case a journey of two miles. I used to pray that I wouldn't meet anyone, but of course I always did. For anyone who has never met pig swill, it consisted of old tea leaves, milk (often curdled), bits of bread, stale cabbage – you name it, everything was in that tin, and often kept for a week before I was sent to collect it! Do you wonder I can smell it still?

I can't remember how long the pigs were kept, but came the day when they were judged to be the right weight, always measured in 'scores', a 'score' being twenty pounds. It was time to send for Mr. May, the slaughterman. What followed next I prefer not to remember. The next day Mr. May came back and jointed the now 'pork'. Relatives and friends got joints sized according to their swill contributions: the rest was salted and stored in a large wooden tub, known as a 'kieve'.

For the first few days we seemed to eat liver and other offal at every meal – I suppose that couldn't be salted, and of course no fridges. The pig's head became brawn, and the excess fat was put into the oven to liquidise and become lard, with the remaining crispy bits being eaten with bread and salt:

the first pork scratchings? I hated them then, and see no reason to change my mind!

Two Loos – Long Trek

Tom's grandma's loo was built at the bottom of the garden, not unusual in those pre-second World War days, but with one very important difference; the seat was positioned directly over a fast-flowing stream, making it probably the first WC in Quarry Close, Nanpean! I'm told it was very efficient, but draughty in winter: and at what cost, I wonder to local Health and Safety? It was possibly still in use in the fifties or sixties.

The loo at our first 'country cottage' was not only way, way up a lane, but in a garden shared with another family; not ideal for a very shy 21 year old. I would wait as long as humanly possible, then make a red-faced dash up the lane. One day I did my usual slink out of the door, good, no-one in sight; quick sprint up the lane, inside loo, slam door. Thank God! Came a whistling up the garden path, so I took a peep out of the grille above the loo door, to see our garden-sharing neighbour happily digging his plot, and obviously prepared for a lengthy stay. No way could I make myself walk past him, so there I sat for a beautiful sunny afternoon while he planted his potatoes.

And from the Ashes Arose a Phoenix

I didn't even know it was happening, the night our church burned down. I was safely tucked up in bed when my husband returned from working the night shift and said "The church is in flames" and so it was.

Perched on its hilltop, the flames were rising hundreds of feet; sheets of scarlet against the black night sky. The firemen did their very, very best – for most of them it was their church too: but by morning only the shell remained. No roof, the beautiful interior reduced to ash, the parishioners reduced to tears.

I have so many memories of that sad time; the weary volunteers who worked day after day, week after week to clear the rubble. The sight of a helicopter flying in the new roof timbers – it was the only way they could be put in place. But the most poignant, the never to be forgotten memory, is of the villagers gathering together on the Church green; no barriers between them. People of all branches of religion, some with no faith at all, and others who weren't quite sure.

It seemed that every soul in the village had come to sing, to pray and to grieve together. Yes, there were many tears, but also the resolve that our church would rise again: and so it has. Different, yes: the ornate rafters have gone, the organ too, but it is still beautiful.

The building welcomes you, enfolds you and gives you peace. It is our church and we love it.

My Beautiful Village

I said to someone the other day "Of course we can't say St. Dennis is a beautiful village" and was about to say "It's a bit grey and austere looking, a typical industrial village" before going on to say why I loved it; but I was stopped with (more in sorrow than anger!) "I wouldn't say that!"

Well, I still think St. Dennis is not your actual picture-postcard village. Its beauty lies in its people; the people who look after each other, the people who comfort you when you are sad and laugh with you when you are happy.

St. Dennis has so many organisations that a full set of fingers and toes is not enough to count them, and our citizens support them all. In sunshine they come, in storm they come, often spending money that has been so hard-earned.

A walk through the village is a joy, with greetings radiating from all directions. It matters not whether you were born here or have migrated, all are welcome here.

Yes, my friend, you were right. St. Dennis IS a beautiful village.